
AN ECUMENICAL LITURGY

A Christian
Celebration of Marriage

The Consultation on Common Texts

FORTRESS PRESS   PHILADELPHIA

Pages 27–32 may be duplicated and used without the permission of the copyright holder or of the publisher, Fortress Press.

Copyright © 1987 by Hans C. Boehringer

Library of Congress Cataloging-in-Publication Data

A Christian celebration of marriage.

1. Marriage service. I. Consultation on Common Texts (Association)
BV199.M3C54   1987   265'.5   86–25831
ISBN 0–8006–1973–0

2672I86   Printed in the United States of America   1–1973

CONSULTATION ON COMMON TEXTS

The Consultation on Common Texts (CCT) originated in the mid-1960s as a forum for consultation on worship renewal among many of the major Christian churches in the United States and Canada. At present, participants in the CCT include persons from the following churches or church agencies:

The American Lutheran Church, Anglican Church of Canada, Christian Church (Disciples of Christ), Episcopal Church, International Commission on English in the Liturgy (representing the Roman Catholic Church in Canada and the United States), Lutheran Church in America, Lutheran Church—Missouri Synod, Presbyterian Church (U.S.A.), Presbyterian Church of Canada, Reformed Church in America, Unitarian Universalist Christian Fellowship, United Church of Canada, United Church of Christ, United Methodist Church.

Projects and publications sponsored by the Consultation on Common Texts include the following:

Prayers We Have in Common. This project sought to provide a contemporary and ecumenical English translation of prayers in regular use by the churches. Initiated by the CCT, it became part of the work of the International Consultation on English Texts.

A Liturgical Psalter for the Christian Year. Growing out of a early study of the liturgical use of psalms, this was prepared and edited by Dr. Massey H. Shepherd, Jr., with the assistance of the CCT. It was published jointly by the Augsburg Publishing House and The Liturgical Press in 1976.

Ecumenical Services of Prayer. This was a result of desire expressed by various members of the CCT to have a simple resource for worship in common on those occasions when Christians of various traditions gather for meetings or celebrations of an ecumenical nature. It was published by the Paulist Press in 1983.

Common Lectionary: The Lectionary Proposed by the Consultation on Common Texts. In order to achieve even greater unity in worship, the CCT has proposed a harmonization of denominational variants in the lectionary for the Sundays and major feast days of the Christian year, based on the three-year lectionary systems now in use in most of the churches in North America. Published by The Church Hymnal Corporation in 1983, this project is being evaluated by the churches.

The present ecumenical liturgy of marriage arises out of concerns for an increasingly common pastoral situation in the churches of North America, and draws upon the considerable unity among the churches regarding both the understanding of marriage and its liturgical celebration.

INTRODUCTION AND PASTORAL NOTES

Marriage between men and women of different Christian churches is relatively common in Canada and the United States of America, and such ecumenical marriages (sometimes also called "inter-church" or "mixed" marriages) provide both opportunities and challenges. Some of the questions raised concern the wedding itself: What church will it be in? How might the clergy of both churches participate and interact? Will the service or liturgy be that of one or the other church or some combination of these? How can it help to further Christian unity and not widen present divisions? and so on. Fortunately, dialogue among the churches shows that they share to a large extent a common understanding of the basic features of marriage.

As a contribution to the pastoral ministry of the churches to those entering into ecumenical marriages, the Consultation on Common Texts (CCT) has prepared *A Christian Celebration of Marriage: An Ecumenical Liturgy*. It is ecumenical, first, in being prepared and endorsed by the CCT, which is an ecumenical body concerned with liturgical matters. In addition, it is ecumenical in being drawn from or based upon the wedding liturgies of these churches. Finally, it has been prepared with ecumenical marriages in mind.

A Christian Celebration of Marriage: An Ecumenical Liturgy is intended for baptized and practicing Christians. Furthermore, the bride and bridegroom are viewed as the primary ministers of the wedding, the ordained clergy having the role of official witnesses and presiders over the liturgical celebration. Members of the family or of the wedding party may appropriately proclaim the Scriptures or serve in other liturgical ministries. This marriage service is to be a communal celebration of the whole gathered community, which represents the whole church in support and prayer. The full participation of all is envisioned. It is also assumed that the wedding will take place in the church of one of the couple.

It is anticipated that an ordained minister of the church in which the wedding is celebrated will act as "host presiding minister," and that he or she will have primary responsibility for the preparation and celebration of the wedding. It is hoped that an ordained minister of the church of the other member of the couple will also participate as "guest presiding minister" or in some other ministerial role. Exactly how the parts of the service are shared by the two ordained ministers needs to be worked out by them together with the couple, and in accord with the customs and disciplines of the two churches. For this reason the rubrics of the service frequently say simply, "A minister says . . ."

The "host presiding minister" is responsible for the proper preparation of the bride and bridegroom for the celebration of the marriage service and for their entry into the state of matrimony. This preparation should include discussion of the marriage liturgy itself; the proper disposition of spirit, mind, heart, and body for marriage; and such other things which experience, wisdom, and the religious traditions involved require. It is highly desirable that the "guest presiding minister" participate in this preparation. The text of *A Christian Celebration of Marriage: An Ecumenical Liturgy* and the Scripture readings it suggests should be an integral part of this preparation.

Though this service fulfills civil law in most places, and the canonical requirements of most churches, it is the responsibility of the clergy involved to make whatever adaptations that may be necessary to fulfill these requirements in particular circumstances. For example, when a priest of the Episcopal Church or Anglican Church of Canada witnesses the vows, the officially approved text of that church is used; other churches may have similar requirements.

Where customary, the banns should be announced on one or more Sundays at the liturgical gatherings of both of the congregations from which the bride and bridegroom come. The forms appropriate to the traditions of the congregations may be used, or this form: "(Name) and (Name) have announced their intention to marry on (Date) at (Place), and ask your prayers."

The core of the service consists of the Word of God followed by the marriage vows. To these are added the other customary elements of wedding liturgies: the exchange of rings, the proclamation of the marriage, and then prayers of intercession and of blessing.

Some elements that had their origins in the betrothal ceremony that once preceded the wedding by some months are placed prior to the Word; their function is to establish the partners' intention to marry and their freedom legally to do so. These betrothal elements, which are used in full in some churches, and omitted or much abbreviated in others, are in this service so arranged in order to separate what is preliminary from what is central. These elements, however, do serve to identify the couple, to allow them to state their intention publicly, and to allow the church community to hear this statement of their intentions.

This service may be set within the eucharistic liturgy (Holy Communion, Lord's Supper) with only slight modification. The discipline of the two churches involved regarding eucharistic sharing should be taken into account in considering this possibility. Within the Eucharist, *A Christian Celebration of Marriage: An Ecumenical Liturgy* should be used as presented here until after the Prayer of Blessing; the Kiss of Peace follows immediately, while the Lord's Prayer and Dismissal take the places usually assigned to them in a eucharistic liturgy.

It is the intention of the Consultation on Common Texts that *A Christian Celebration of Marriage: An Ecumenical Liturgy* be used as presented here. Adaptations may be made, however, when pastorally necessary. In particular circumstances, for example, the Affirmation by Families may have to be modified or omitted.

Music, because of its capacity to heighten our sense of celebration, is an important part of the marriage rite. The texts used should direct the worshipers toward the praise of God and the love God has for men and women. Texts that direct the attention of the worshipers primarily to the love between the bride and bridegroom generally do not meet this criterion. Music drawn from the world of theater and entertainment likewise is generally not appropriate for use within the service itself. Music and texts that are not suitable for use within the worship of the gathered assembly may in many instances be quite appropriately used at other times when family and friends are gathered to celebrate the marriage.

The Consultation of Common Texts asks the God and Father of our Lord Jesus Christ to bless those who use *A Christian Celebration of Marriage: An Ecumenical Liturgy* with peace, true happiness, and holiness.

ORDER OF SERVICE

GATHERING
> Greeting
> (Questions to the Congregation and the Couple)
> Public Declaration of Intention
> Affirmation by Families and Congregation
> Prayer of the Day

WORD OF GOD

THE MARRIAGE
> Marriage Vows
> Exchange of Rings
> Announcement of the Marriage

PRAYERS
> Prayers of Intercession
> Prayer of Blessing
> Lord's Prayer

CONCLUSION
> Kiss of Peace
> Dismissal

Portions in brackets are optional.
Texts said by the congregation are in **bold face.**
Music is suggested as a preference or as an option in the following places:
> At the Gathering
> The Psalm following the First Reading
> Following the Sermon
> Following the Announcement of the Marriage
> At the Dismissal

GATHERING

The people gather, forming a community of friends of the couple, in order to offer thanks to God, to serve as witnesses, and to assure the couple of their continuing support and love.

It is important that hospitality be shown to welcome all those who are not part of the local congregation.

The congregation stands.

The ministers enter and go to the entrance of the church to welcome the wedding party.

After they have greeted the bride and bridegroom, the entire party enters the church and goes to a place in front of the assembly. The procession may take this order: Cross and torches, assisting ministers, host and guest presiding ministers, attendants, parents, and bride and bridegroom.

It is appropriate that a hymn or psalm be sung during the entrance, or music may be performed by instrumentalists or a choir.

[If a simpler entrance is desired, the ministers come before the assembly. The bride, bridegroom, and their attendants enter the church together and stand before the ministers and the assembly.]

GREETING

A minister says:
The grace of our Lord Jesus Christ, the love of God,
and the communion of the Holy Spirit be with you all.
And also with you.

Dear friends:
We have come together in the presence of God
to witness the marriage of (Name) and (Name),
to surround them with our prayers,
and to share in their joy.

10

The Scriptures teach us that the bond and covenant of marriage is a
   gift of God,
a holy mystery in which man and woman become one flesh,
an image of the union of Christ and the church.

As this man and this woman give themselves to each other today,
we remember that at Cana in Galilee our Lord Jesus Christ
made the wedding feast a sign of God's kingdom of love.

Let us enter into this celebration confident that,
through the Holy Spirit, Christ is present with us now also;
we pray that this couple may fulfill God's purpose
for the whole of their lives.

If required by law or local custom:

QUESTIONS TO THE CONGREGATION AND THE COUPLE
A minister says to the congregation:
These two persons have come here to become one in this holy
union. But if any of you can show just cause why they may not
lawfully be married, declare it now or hereafter remain silent.

A minister says to the couple:
(Name) and (Name), have you come here freely and without reser-
vation to join together lawfully in marriage?

The bride and bridegroom separately respond:
I have.

PUBLIC DECLARATION OF INTENTION
A minister says to the bride:
(Name),
will you have (Name) to be your husband,
to live together in a holy marriage?
Will you love him, comfort him,
honor and keep him,
in sickness and in health,
and, forsaking all others,
be faithful to him as long as you both shall live?

11

The bride responds:
I will.

A minister says to the bridegroom:
(Name),
will you have (Name) to be your wife,
to live together in a holy marriage?
Will you love her, comfort her,
honor and keep her,
in sickness and in health,
and, forsaking all others,
be faithful to her as long as you both shall live?

The bridegroom responds:
I will.

AFFIRMATION BY FAMILIES AND CONGREGATION

A minister says to the families:
Do you, the families of (Name) and (Name),
give your love and blessing to this new family?
We do.

Members of the families may share expressions of encouragement and love with the couple.

A minister says to the congregation:
Will all of you, by God's grace, do everything in your power to uphold and care for these two persons in their life together?
We will.

PRAYER OF THE DAY

A minister says:
Let us pray.

Gracious God,
you sent your Son Jesus Christ into the world

12

A CHRISTIAN CELEBRATION OF MARRIAGE—ERRATA SHEET

Insert at the top of page 13:

to reveal your love to all people.
Enrich these your servants with every good gift,

that their life together may show forth your love;
and grant that at the last we may all celebrate with Christ
the marriage feast which has no ending.
In the Name of Jesus Christ our Lord.
Amen.

The congregation is seated.

WORD OF GOD

Suggested Bible readings are given on pages 23–25. Three (or two) readings may be chosen, one of which is always from the Gospels.

Before the First Reading, the reader may say:
A reading from (the name of the book of the Bible).
First Reading (see below)

At the conclusion of the First Reading, the reader may say:
The word of the Lord.
And the congregation may respond:
Thanks be to God.

A psalm or hymn is sung as a response to the First Reading.
Psalm (see below)

Before the Second Reading, the reader may say:
A reading from (the name of the book of the Bible).
Second Reading (see below)

At the conclusion of the Second Reading, the reader may say:
The word of the Lord.
And the congregation may respond:
Thanks be to God.

An acclamation (Alleluia) or hymn may be sung as a preparation for the Gospel.
All may stand for the Gospel.

Before the Gospel, the minister who reads it may say:
The Holy Gospel of our Lord Jesus Christ
according to (the name of the Gospel).
And the congregation may respond:
Glory to you, O Lord.

Gospel (see below)

At the conclusion of the Gospel, the minister may say:
The Gospel of the Lord.

And the congregation may respond:
Praise to you, Lord Jesus Christ.

The congregation is seated.

A Sermon or Homily is then preached.
  Sermon or Homily

A hymn may be sung.

THE MARRIAGE

(The congregation is seated.)

The bride and bridegroom stand in view of the congregation, and face each other.

A minister says:
Join your hands and declare your vows.

The bride and bridegroom join their hands
and speak so that all can hear.
The minister discreetly helps the couple proclaim their vows.
The bridegroom says:
In the presence of God and this community,
I, (Name), take you, (Name),
to be my wife;
to have and to hold from this day forward,
in joy and in sorrow,
in plenty and in want,
in sickness and in health,
to love and to cherish,
as long as we both shall live.
This is my solemn vow.

The bride says:
In the presence of God and this community,
I, (Name), take you, (Name),
to be my husband;
to have and to hold from this day forward,
in joy and in sorrow,
in plenty and in want,
in sickness and in health,
to love and to cherish,

16

as long as we both shall live.
This is my solemn vow.

EXCHANGE OF RINGS

It is preferable that two rings be exchanged.
The rings are placed on a suitable plate, or on the service book of
the minister, or are held by an assisting minister.

A minister says:
Bless, O Lord, [the giving of] these rings;
may they who wear them
live in love and fidelity,
and continue in your service
all the days of their lives,
through Jesus Christ our Lord.
Amen.

[If only one ring is exchanged:
Bless, O Lord, [the giving of] this ring;
may *he* who gives it and *she* who wears it
live in love and fidelity,
and continue in your service
all the days of their lives,
through Jesus Christ our Lord.
Amen.]

The bridegroom places the ring on the ring finger of the bride, and
speaks so that all can hear:
(Name), I give you this ring,
as a sign of the covenant we have made today.
[In the Name of the Father, Son, and Holy Spirit.]

The bride places the ring on the ring finger of the bridegroom, and
speaks so that all can hear:
(Name), I give you this ring,
as a sign of the covenant we have made today.
[In the Name of the Father, Son, and Holy Spirit.]

[If only one ring is exchanged, the appropriate omission is made.]

17

If it is customary, other suitable tokens may be exchanged or used at this time.

ANNOUNCEMENT OF THE MARRIAGE

A minister says:
Now that (Name) and (Name)
have given themselves to each other
by solemn vows,
with the joining of hands,
and the giving of rings,
I announce to you that they are husband and wife.

Those whom God has joined together,
let no one put asunder.

Blessed be the Lord our God now and forever. Amen.

A hymn may be sung.

PRAYERS

The congregation stands.

A minister says:
Friends of Christ,
in the midst of our joy
let us also pray for this broken world.

For all people in their daily life and work;
for our families, friends, neighbors,
and for all whose lives touch ours.
We pray to you, our God.

For this holy fellowship of faith
  in which we seek your grace;
For the world, the nation, and this community,
  in which we work for justice, freedom, and peace.
We pray to you, our God.

For the just and proper use of your creation;
for the victims of hunger, injustice, and oppression.
We pray to you, our God.

For all who are in danger, sorrow, or any kind of trouble;
for those who minister to the sick, the friendless,
and the needy.
We pray to you, our God.

For those who have suffered the loss of child or parent, husband or
  wife;
for those to whom love is a stranger.
We pray to you, our God.

19

Most gracious God,
you have made us in your own image
and given us over to one another's care.
Hear the prayers of your people,
that unity may overcome division,
hope vanquish despair,
and joy conquer sorrow.
Through Jesus Christ our Lord.
Amen.

PRAYER OF BLESSING

The couple may kneel.

A minister says:
Blessed are you, Lord God, Heavenly Father.
In your great love you created us male and female
and made the union of husband and wife
an image of the covenant between you and your people.
You sent Jesus Christ to come among us,
making your love visible in him,
to bring new life to the world.

Send your Holy Spirit to pour out
the abundance of your blessing on (Name) and (Name),
who have this day given themselves
to each other in marriage.

Bless them in their work and in their companionship;
in their sleeping and in their waking;
in their joys and in their sorrows;
in their life and in their death.

(Give them the gift and heritage of children
in accordance with your will,
and make their home a haven of peace.)
Let their love for each other be a seal upon their hearts,
a mantle about their shoulders,
and a crown upon their foreheads.

Bless them so that all may see in their lives together
in the community of your people
a vision of your kingdom on earth.
And finally, in the fullness of time,
welcome them into the glory of your presence.
Through your Son Jesus Christ
with the Holy Spirit in your holy church
all honor and glory is yours, Almighty Father,
now and for ever.
Amen.

LORD'S PRAYER

A minister says:
And now, with the confidence of children of God, let us pray:

Our Father in heaven,
  hallowed be your name,
  your kingdom come,
  your will be done,
  on earth as in heaven.
Give us today our daily bread.
Forgive us our sins
  as we forgive those
  who sin against us.
Save us from the time of trial
  and deliver us from evil.
For the kingdom, the power,
  and the glory are yours,
  now and forever. Amen.

The couple rises.

CONCLUSION

KISS OF PEACE

The husband and wife may greet each other with a kiss.
Greetings may be exchanged throughout the congregation.

DISMISSAL

A minister says:
The Lord bless you and keep you.
The Lord make his face shine on you
and be gracious to you.
The Lord look upon you with favor
and give you peace.
Amen.

A minister says:
Go in peace to love and serve the Lord.
Thanks be to God.

The wedding party then leaves the church.
A hymn, psalm, or choral music may be sung,
or instrumental music may be played.

BIBLE READINGS

In some cases more than one chapter and verse reference is given for a particular reading; this reflects the usages of different churches.

Readings may be made either from a Bible or a Lectionary.

FIRST READING

The creation of man and woman
  Genesis 1:26-28, 31a [Genesis 1:26-28]
The creation of woman
  Genesis 2:18-24 [Genesis 2:4-9, 15-24]
Love is strong as death
  Song of Songs 2:8-10, 14, 16a; 8:6-7a
  [Songs of Songs 2:10-13 or 2:8-13; 8:6-7]
The new covenant of the people of God
  Jeremiah 31:31-32a, 33-34a [Jeremiah 31:31-34]
The love of God
  Isaiah 54:5-8
The betrothal of God and Israel
  Hosea 2:16-23

The marriage of Tobias and Sarah
  Tobit 7:9c-10, 11c-17
Prayer of the new spouses
  Tobit 8:4-9 [Tobit 8:5-9]
A good wife
  Ecclesiasticus (Sirach) 26:1-4, 16-21

PSALM

One of the following psalms is used as a response following the First Reading. If possible it is to be sung. An appropriate hymn may also be used.

Psalm 23
Psalm 33 [Psalm 33:12, 18, 20–21, 22]
Psalm 34 [Psalm 34:2–9]
Psalm 37:3–7
Psalm 67
Psalm 100
Psalm 103 [Psalm 103:1–2, 8, 13, 17–18a]
Psalm 112 [Psalm 112:1–9]
Psalm 117
Psalm 121
Psalm 127
Psalm 128 [Psalm 128:1–5]
Psalm 136
Psalm 145 [Psalm 145:8–10, 15, 17–18]
Psalm 148 [Psalm 148:1–4, 9–14]
Psalm 150

SECOND READING

The love of Christ
  Romans 8:31b–35, 37–39 [Romans 8:31b–39]
The life of a Christian
  Romans 12:1–2, 9–18 [Romans 12:1–2, 9–13]
Your members are temples of the Holy Spirit
  1 Corinthians 6:13c–15a, 17–19
  [1 Corinthians 6:15–20]
The greatest of these is love
  1 Corinthians 12:31—13:8a
  [1 Corinthians 13:1–13]
The love of Christ
  Ephesians 3:14–21
The mystery of marriage
  Ephesians 5:2a, 21–33
Live in love and thanksgiving

Colossians 3:12-17
Peace and harmony in the family
1 Peter 3:1-9
Love is real and active
1 John 3:18-24
God is love
1 John 4:7-12 [1 John 4:7-16]
The wedding feast of the Lamb
Revelation 19:1, 5-9a

GOSPEL

The beatitudes
Matthew 5:1-12a [Matthew 5:1-10]
Salt of the earth and light of the world
Matthew 5:13-16
House built upon a rock
Matthew 7:21, 24-29
What God has united must not be divided
Matthew 19:3-6
Love, the greatest commandment
Matthew 22:35-40
Two become one body
Mark 10:6-9 [Mark 10:6-9, 13-16]
Marriage feast of Cana
John 2:1-11
Remain in my love
John 15:9-12 [John 15:9-17]

AN ECUMENICAL LITURGY

A Christian
Celebration of Marriage

The Consultation on Common Texts

The Consultation on Common Texts is a forum for consultation on worship renewal among many of the major Christian churches in the United States and Canada. Participants in the Consultation include persons from the following churches or church agencies:

The American Lutheran Church, Anglican Church of Canada, Christian Church (Disciples of Christ), Episcopal Church, International Commission on English in the Liturgy (representing the Roman Catholic Church in Canada and the United States), Lutheran Church in America, Lutheran Church —Missouri Synod, Presbyterian Church (U.S.A.), Presbyterian Church of Canada, Reformed Church in America, Unitarian Universalist Christian Fellowship, United Church of Canada, United Church of Christ, United Methodist Church.

GATHERING

*(The people are invited to respond as indicated in **boldface**.)*
The congregation stands as the bridal party and ministers enter.
Entrance hymn or instrumental music.

GREETING

The grace of our Lord Jesus Christ, the love of God, and the communion of the Holy Spirit be with you all.
And also with you.
Dear friends: We have come together in the presence of God . . .
. . . we pray that this couple may fulfill God's purpose for the whole of their lives.

PUBLIC DECLARATION OF INTENTION

(The couple declare their intention to marry.)

AFFIRMATION BY FAMILIES
AND CONGREGATION

Minister: Do you, the families of N and N, give your love and blessing to this new family?
Families: **We do.**

Minister: Will all of you, by God's grace, do everything in your power to uphold and care for these two persons in their life together?
All: **We will.**

PRAYER OF THE DAY

Let us pray . . .
Amen.
The congregation is seated.

THE WORD OF GOD

FIRST READING

The reader may conclude: "The word of the Lord."
Thanks be to God.
(A psalm or hymn is sung as a response to the Reading.)

SECOND READING

The reader may conclude: "The word of the Lord."
Thanks be to God.

THE GOSPEL

(An acclamation or hymn may be sung as a preparation for the Gospel.)
Before the Gospel, the minister who reads it may say:
"The Holy Gospel of our Lord Jesus Christ . . ."
Glory to you, O Lord.
The minister may conclude: "The Gospel of the Lord."
Praise to you, Lord Jesus Christ.
The congregation is seated.

SERMON OR HOMILY

A hymn may be sung.

THE MARRIAGE

(The congregation is seated.)

MARRIAGE VOWS

BLESSING AND
EXCHANGE OF RINGS

Bless, O Lord, (the giving of) these rings . . .
. . . through Jesus Christ our Lord.
Amen.

ANNOUNCEMENT OF THE MARRIAGE

Now that (Name) and (Name) have given themselves . . .
Those whom God has joined together, let no one put asunder.
Blessed be the Lord our God now and forever. Amen.
A hymn may be sung.

PRAYERS

The congregation stands.

PRAYERS OF INTERCESSION

The response to the Prayers is:
We pray to you, our God.
Most gracious God . . .
Amen.

PRAYER OF BLESSING

Blessed are you, Lord God . . .
. . . and glory is yours, Almighty Father, now and for ever.
Amen.

LORD'S PRAYER

Our Father in heaven,
hallowed be your name,
your kingdom come,
your will be done,
on earth as in heaven.
Give us today our daily bread.
Forgive us our sins
as we forgive those who sin against us.
Save us from the time of trial
and deliver us from evil.
For the kingdom, the power, and the glory are yours,
now and forever. Amen.

CONCLUSION

KISS OF PEACE

The Sign of Peace may be exchanged throughout the congregation.

DISMISSAL

The Lord bless you and keep you . . .
Amen.
Go in peace to love and serve the Lord.
Thanks be to God.
(Concluding hymn, choral, or instrumental music.)